LOVE THE STRANGER

JAY DESHPANDE

LOVE THE STRANGER

YESYES BOOKS

COVER ART: "ANTONYM" COURTESY OF THE ARTIST
AND MARIANNE BOESKY GALLERY, NEW YORK
© DIANA AL-HADID, PHOTO CREDIT: JASON WYCHE
COVER AND INTERIOR DESIGN BY ALBAN FISCHER

FIRST EDITION, 2015
ISBN 978-1-936919-33-8
PRINTED IN THE UNITED STATES OF AMERICA

PUBLISHED BY YESYES BOOKS
4904 NE 29TH AVE
PORTLAND, OR 97211
YESYESBOOKS.COM

KMA SULLIVAN, PUBLISHER
HEATHER BROWN, PUBLICIST
MARK DERKS, FICTION EDITOR, VINYL
STEVIE EDWARDS, ACQUISITIONS EDITOR
ALBAN FISCHER, GRAPHIC DESIGNER
JILL KOLONGOWSKI, MANAGING EDITOR
JAMIE MORTARA, WEB DESIGN AND MANAGEMENT
BEYZA OZER, DEPUTY DIRECTOR OF SOCIAL MEDIA
AMBER RAMBHAROSE, CREATIVE DIRECTOR OF SOCIAL MEDIA
PHILLIP B. WILLIAMS, POETRY EDITOR, VINYL
JOANN BALINGIT, ASSISTANT EDITOR
MARY CATHERINE CURLEY, ASSISTANT EDITOR
ASHLEY C. FORD, CONTRIBUTING EDITOR, VINYL
LEWIS MUNDT, ASSISTANT EDITOR
CARLY SCHWEPPE, INTERN, VINYL
HARI ZIYAD, ASSISTANT EDITOR, VINYL

FOR MY FAMILY, ALWAYS BECOMING

CONTENTS

LOVE THE STRANGER

APOLOGIA PRO VITA SUA

We don't have much time so we have to work
slowly. We unwrap the small
almost-animal form until it whimpers
under the heat of our gaze. We put the books
up on the shelf; we take them back down again.
At evening, chin back and the neck
like a skyscraper, we give up smoke—a colony
of ghost-howl. Color of light
that collects on rooftops, with desire
propped like a water tower in the corner:
each day ends in the labor of small hands
through delicate hair. I remember a time
with a woman I knew only as the sound of her hair.
After we had both come and spent ourselves
on the smells of each other, we went up on the roof
and lay down on my coat, wishing
that people could see the stars in this city.
And I remember how I slipped into sleep for a moment
and was back by the hayfield of my boyhood
with my brother, crickets sparking in the failing sun
that paced out beyond us and burnished the tips
of the nearest pines. How the edge of that forest
was only slightly farther away. But I never touched it.
It seems I am always running ahead of my needing,
looking out from a higher window of the body
to see the edges of things, the weight
of a pound of grapes in my hand, that tactile rush

of consolation. But I am here now.
I am resting my head against the part of myself
I am willing to put down.
Why didn't we enter that field?
Why didn't we cross to that border, Neil, to see
what it felt like to push the first foot down
into the shadow and the cooler ferns?
At night, my breath slacks into darkness
and I feel the air winnow through my arm.
I am beginning to see how I am that field,
that moment pushing sunset, blank distance to the treeline,
how the woods at the end of me are porous, giving,
how they shimmer on air.
The roots are moving, out of sight.
The crickets singing through me.
Tonight I will sleep like a just man,
a good man, a man who has hurt others
in order to lay his head down.

DOWN

PRAIRIE SONG WITH JACK PALANCE

Enough times now I've dropped the blade of love
in the lake, thumb scrambling moon on the surface
to find again the hilt, and catch there. It's very dark here,
and my palms come up slashed faintly with language
I can't read until I've made the fire. Then I see it all:
summer mornings spanning out impossibly
the shape your back left in the dust on the table
how an angel wades into water to keep his wings dry
and that name, like the light of the moon on a coyote's coat.
Someone's hand still hovers above the holstered butt
of midnight. Little rivulets through red clay forming
a continent of blood. How I crossed the plains for you,
for your clothes like cottonwoods, for this cliff
of squint. Men die in just a little less air than this,
a little less breath. I get a feeling that comes out of the clouds
on a ghost with veins and reins to wrap its hands.
I know what I'm entitled to, it's this vision I keep past stars
of a cowboy name. At times it whistles through the canyons.

FOREST : TREES

What were you doing in the tall grass and did it work for you,
did you find your hectic maker,
did she cause you great trouble, or did she touch you

with her leaf-covered hands and her hands made of twigs?
Was she gentle, her horns gentle,
did she make of you a gentle planet? Some loves are too much for words

but you speak them. You lay down in the grass, you befriended
the grass, you composed a short lecture and pronounced it
to the trees. *i. The weekend is a system of cadenzas. ii. If I spend*

enough time observing the kitchen counter, I'll become the kitchen counter.
iii. Have you heard the one about the man who walks into town at thirty-five
with nothing but a letter and no name and no voice?

Laughter whinges in the saplings.
Now you come back to your hectic,
and she provides for you, to the nostrils. For your mind

let the head of a dead deer. For the bridge you would build
through the dark, select tools. (One of them the shape of your hand.)
It's okay, you can go ahead: to the butterfly caught in the airshaft,

whisper *I've got to see you again*. When you pull yourself up
off the edge call it morning. When you find that you're sick of the dust
call it snow.

AMOR FATI

I am trying to understand. I have washed
clean the canopy and set the knives in order.
They lie there on the bed like a ladder.
I let August pass over me like news
in smaller fonts. Over and over I am
caught dumb by my face blossoming
out of the mirror in a drunken language.
It wants to tell me something, speak
its one sentence before collapse.
Approaching thirty, it is becoming clear
a man can make the same mistake
many times, in the same clothes, the same
shiver and clutch on the fire escape,
the same brightness in the white exhale.
How many times did I wake up next to her
only to wake up again. Lately, I have confidence
in laundry. I trust the café on the corner, rude
edges of an old brown book, or the basic
way I masturbate, eyes on the roofline
of a house three blocks away. In half-light
I know what song brings every one of us
here, it goes: refrain, refrain, refrain.
But we will never have enough
of being wrong about the other, not once.

She turned away from me to the window.
I was still breathing hard. *And you're
hurting me like this* I wanted to say
but I couldn't speak in that darkness.
The line of her half-dressed body
on its side. She smoothed her hair.
"But a sari is the most incredible,"
she whispered. (She had that about her,
to just keep going. None of my actions
could stop that river of talk.) "Because
you always know with a single pull
the five yards of fabric could just
fall away." I had no strength.
I lunged for her.

THE SECRET LIFE

August unfolded but remembrance
like the tongues of prisoners
like the air blurred thicker
after a hot bath
and the bent wire
outside the window
legs of a black horse
moving far away
and the prayers in the dark
of young girls listening
to wind rustle the wheat fields
green and blue

INFLORESCENCE

I don't know what's happening in the north woods
but passion its black fruit you pluck and crawl inside,
feeling in its clutch the power one day meant
to sing and flower inside of your face
like a klaxon. At any rate, I didn't ring it.
Have you ever felt so close to someone you reached
for the place where your thumb would press
to peel back their skin? Around the table
moralities gather. I'll stay here thank you
I am staying here thank you.
Among trees you never release yourself.
You just stay by the water, ghostly plea,
quick glance at the moss. It becomes slowly clear
you haven't yet found anything you like.
Other things becoming clear. All day
you walk ten feet in front of you
and the human brain is only a conversation.
The human brain is only a conversation
try something different for a change. Someone's cold lungs
are speaking to me directly now. Somebody's
feet gather together to form a sudden cliff.
Every firstborn child named precipice.
I say crawl inside you, and crawl inside you.

THE LOVERS

When I reached for her for the first time
what we groped toward had already
unmade itself. The barstool crashes down
and we are back outside, deaf to nearly everything.
She starts speaking her words on my face
but I stop her. Bare legs and skirt
pressed up against the side of a car,
at the side of a street, familiar story.
A hunger become so animal I can't see
the shape of the hole. What it took for me
to lie down in the brief wreckage
of our lives. Like a drop of blood into water
I watched the loss spread out, heralding
some reaction. I live quietly now,
by myself, mildly hallucinating.
In Magritte's *The Lovers*, it's a dream
seduction: figures locked in profile
in a kiss you cannot see. Shadow
where the faces meet, and there are no faces:
only the two, man and woman, held apart
by the colorless cloth covering
the head of each. Sculptural folds of
the permanent kiss, which isn't.
I had an idea that one shroud
held them both, one sheet like the garment
over furniture in a country house,
that same indifferent smock, only tighter

for the strictures of love. The sheet wrapped
double about his neck and pulled around
to hers, kept off the bare shoulder. That place
where you can imagine her chin. What part
of us must stay under a separate cloth? There is
something uncommunicated in Magritte.
Perhaps I go to that. My hand
on her wrist, my hand showing
her the way to me, guiding her
down a street where I have never
opened my eyes. Behind those painted figures
a storm, without center, rising.
How they ever found their way to each other.

THE PORTENT OF SILENCE

At times, brief times, it comes in like song.
And I was raised incredulous to quiet.

I don't want to be disbelieved of the fact of a pronoun
or the necessary confrontation in a name. I undress

the castle waiting for me eventual
in my unevenness. A hole stays in the place

I look, fondling clouds out the backseat window
of a slow late ride to what was home. But I won't go home.

A woman rises out of the clavicle of my apology.
An artillery going about sunset all the wrong ways

and I can't behave. When I say Chet Baker I mean
I have been with my shepherd a little longer

than required, perhaps a problem because
I like it there. Ask the voice to come back thick

with the blood of the air, my muted human hum
feathered over high hills. But I cannot have it yet.

EXORDIUM

What can I put beside you,
what can I rest on you, you
who are filling the cup at an angle and
always? There are still those uncut pages
in the journal of my deeds. Words held
to words by the hot parts of their own making.
I keep an adhesive love for the great
fictions of this century. *You're in awe*
you're still in awe they say. They say *You*
have felt it all and yet you float
on nearer waters. Or, my favorite:
What hurt you will be real money
if you breathe on it, put it back inside you.

REPORTS OF THE DREAM YOU'RE NOT LIKELY TO RECOVER FROM

You know how it goes. You love something dearly,
something that you make with your own two hands,
lovingly, molding the skull, the back of the neck.
That heat only you can feel beneath the chin.

But you don't ever give it a face. Maybe
call it bravery. You remember the green stem gold,
your hands around the neck. How you watched
the sun come up drained of blood. You remember

everything in a timescale of your own design.
Every day your blind hands work on the same project
naming it different things as time goes by
to keep up the frenzied newness of the romance.

Each body plucked out of the tree of night
will be still and dead by morning, then found
in a well of light. But this part's best of all:
when you return to that warmth below the chin you feel

a new correctness, not unlike stupor,
showering you in hot sparks. You feel a hitman's craving
coming on, rounding corners, ready for awakening.
Perhaps it seems a little odd to be so disrobed

by night-music. But you have found a new lover.
Her touch uncertain, her eyes an absence, her skin
the braided violets only seen in sleep.
She is coming for you in a timescale of your own design.

She is lifting her hands like an orchestra.

ON VOLUPTUOUSNESS
AT LA FONTANA DI TREVI

Some part of everything
curves away from you.

STRENGTH

Perfection is terrible, it cannot have children.
—SYLVIA PLATH

Mostly it goes and then it goes
    farther away. A car leaving town
down a dirt road. Remainders in the glib

    afternoon: silt of wine still in the glass,
or echoes of summer motion in curtains
    you can see through. Motion brought about

by nothing but the wind. Soon it billows out
    to months where the night rises like a fence
in the distance, then not the distance, then

    nearer—and the questions keep coming back.
Something half-heard in sleep about the hands,
    about the lion's jaws. Wake up

wondering after love which way gets you
    back to the house alone. Which lie to believe.
Outside some neighbors laugh, children laugh,

    soon they'll be your neighbors. Vessel
passing further. Rush of recalled fire. This
    is what self-control becomes—

we are holding the lion before we want
        to hold the lion, and after, and every
moment in between is unexplained and horrible.

        There is nothing quite so alien as being
correct. Her body rising from the bed, now leaving
        the bed, now far away in another country.

Watch yourself grow muscle in your failures
        and hate it. Warbler mindless jumping
branch to branch. Miles Davis—that was it.

        Near the end of his life he played new songs
every night, harsh ones no one wanted.
        Haze and copper. Neon. Fuzz, or bramble.

People came only for the legend.
        One night he got onstage sick enough
to not know where he was.

        He counted off and started to play—but it was
"My Funny Valentine." And then "I Thought About You."
        And the audience was ecstatic, hearing

what they wanted. After, a young piano player
        peered into his dressing room, found him
hunched before the mirror. Miles looked up.

        "Kid, you know why I never play those songs
no matter how much anyone asks for them?"
        He paused, looking wide at the ceiling

like there was something to prepare for,
someone still to fight.
"It's because I love those songs."

THE GAME OF UNBECOMING

Hair up, mirror-faced, in the light
I can't see from, you pen shadows
underneath your eyes and call me
to my name again. I know
how this one goes, it's the game
of unbecoming, where I'll soon see
several parts of me move outward
under cloudface like those ships
in the harbor we hear from.
I am just lying here another minute
at the thought of those straining hulls,
at the sound in my head
of weird thick ropes
creaking under hysterically
orchestrated moonlight.
There isn't much time left before
my lungs slip away, my laugh slips away
when you've come out from under covers
like that moon, and I'm presumptuous
and horrible enough to think
if I could just put my confidence
in you then maybe
I'd understand.

TRACING

I know what it was:
your body stretched before me like a fence
keeping its shiver and creak, something incredible
as if the forest I grew up beside but could never touch were,
when I blow cool air over my memory, stippled
with fine hairs that stand on end
in a shock of pine.

Some of us are heading to the castle
some of us are too tired for the castle
some of us fade into sleep. Dawn stumbles
down the tree-lined street, gray and sublunary
like a stripped god. Outside
the dank well of barlight, a pale wrist flicks ash
and imagines the orange tip of the cigarette
a castle prepared and waiting. Its citizens know
when the party is over, when repeated dance moves
become as pointless as cars on islands. No one stands up
from our bench in the barlight, rubbing cold knees.
How is it a train so often shudders beneath our feet?
The force it takes to know the organism completely
is starless, is dividing up the tip in even portions and settling
its necktie. Soon I'll be left alone. I'll wish better luck
to the bodies of my future selves, translating
the evening so it can talk to me. *Okay*
the moon looks like a mistake in the sky
they'll say into the hollow bottles of afternoon.
The throat strung out among last daffodils best
knows the daffodils. I am still the surest thing
outside of cabfare. I am still leaving this borough tonight
and entering the castle, by myself if necessary.
I have this game I like to play where I close my eyes
and pretend I'm a blind man, returning
to a city I designed in the years before I lost my sight,

where I should still know every length and walk
in darkness, a trauma unknown and known before.
Here, I play the game again for you.

KLAXON

You who are beside me, who are hearing
my voice tap out the familiar strains
of a devastation we journey toward
and will sleep inside forever, I have seen you
restlessly parading your thoughts on the marble,
your back turned to the hanged man
who blocks out the sun, and every alarm
waiting for the moment when we cry out:
All of it, all of it was given to us,
it was not our choice how the trees
tied knots around our arms, how the summer clenched
resolutely not in love with anything, how we asked
to be instrumental and didn't think we'd get it
but we did, and it's here, and it goes like this.

COMMEMORATION

For seven months he fought himself. He saw
what he had lost. The streets became romantic
and then were hushed with weather.
He tried several manners of speaking,
then put them back down. He pushed away
the obvious. His hand was a comb through fleece.
The city moved around him faster.
There were flies in the morning light. Drunk festivals
forgotten, and more names than he could pick up,
spoken on terraces. After awhile, he didn't believe
that she had been all that he'd said she had been.
He felt a quiet, and sometimes he hated it.
Then a voice came to him and said,
Don't lose your longing: this is what makes you
a willow among willows. You seek a calm
that comes from knowing you have made
only correct choices. But we do not
come here for that. We come here
to press our backs up against the invisible,
to wake up in the night with a cough that becomes
the spring all over again and makes us toss and turn.
We come here for alleviation, but what we're here for
is light. Soon, in a day, in a year, you will be
a blessing again. Your breath a prayer.
And you will know her for what she was to you:
broad bay, rising sun. A truth
you won't run away from. Listen

to those trees saying she will never come back.
She will never come back.
But what you felt extends. It goes on and on.
And you must keep that for as long as you live.
Come, pick up your arrows.
The animals are moving again.

ENTERING THE CASTLE

THREATENING WEATHER

When I woke up in the city
a man was taking me out to eat
in a purple building. On the table
he had arranged upturned
wineglasses, his silver napkin,
the peel of an orange, the contents
of his many pockets. His hands
fluttered over the objects,
placing and replacing them.

Imagine, he said, this is a map
of the center of your mind.
When you are awake it is
at the center. When you are asleep
it is at the center. Only when
you reside in the dead place between
can it slip away. Only then
can you roam around
outside of it, outside the dead
center of your mind.

The hour was not late but his face
was moonlight. The man
would not look up. I asked him
how we knew each other.

We were both born
here, he said, and pointed
to the silver napkin, which trembled
as though a small creature
warm and fearful
cringed beneath its folds.

DRAMATIS PERSONAE or
IN THIS HOUSE A SINGLE THREAD

The Maker of Attachments who laces up his jewelry.

The Fanciful Dresser, with ingenious curls that almost toss themselves, and Her Delicate Suits.

The Harbor-Keeper: he is a keeper of harbors.

The Tree that grows along his spine.

The Knuckles with dirt on them, in a pleasant napping fist, laid on the table. It is dirt it is blood it is dirt.

And the Policeman's Friends boarding the bus at night, the bus kneeling to receive, the Friends finding seats, the lights back out, and the stumbled language they talk in to each other. Like a metal horn grafted on a violin.

The one who Keeps You Occupied.

The one In Shadows Before You Get There.

The one who is Afraid, And So Strongly that your voice answering her question makes her hands tremble over a plate of food.

The Visitor who comes and brings the present of your body.

And the Present of Your Body.

And the Adventurer, and knowing what his name used to be.

The Bus-Driver, we mustn't forget the Bus-Driver.

The Cavernous in your parents' house. The summer day, the almost-touch, then the beach, and more friends, and the Cavernous, how it stays caving.

The Clever Translator—but we keep our eyes on his hands.

The Debtor who cousins to the Maker of Attachments.

The Truck Outside On The Street, and on the street again. The curtain can't expulse it.

You, with your map in your mouth and sometimes for weeks.

Again, that Damned Music from the horn-violin.

The Limb that falls asleep beside the bed that falls asleep beside and it is not your body.

The Limb that blesses you.

The Moon when not.

Him With His Teeth In His Face.

Brother, Brother of Shelves, watching eyes aware all night, drinking from a cup and saying this milk tastes like a game.

All the Pieces sprawled out on the table, and a Voice demanding you put them together.

Those Hours when you try to do so. They go on.

Will he come again, Him With His Teeth In His Face?

The Woman who stops you on the street to ask for money, not for her not for anything, but just to hand it back to you.

And Entanglement in slush.

And the Slush is terrible.

And the Night Imagining, Imagining for days.

PORN

On the screen are a man and a woman. They are watching tv,
a program about the 1965 World's Fair and the animatronic
president at the Illinois pavilion. They become distracted
by bodies: having them, and each other. They begin to undress.
Silk sleeve. An arm wants to be bare, and then it is. His shirt, her
shoulder, pants, pants. A shoe drops to the floor. One face
is on the other's face, then it is somewhere else. Her hand
puts his body into hers. Their eyes close. And still the blue hum
of the tv to wash them. And still the sound of it, heard behind
the groans and gasps: *The trouble was Lincoln was nowhere*
near being operational. The simple system that ran the tiki birds
wasn't advanced enough for Lincoln. To make him seem human
would need a far more complex mechanism; and it would have
to be packed into a very small space: Lincoln's skull, to be precise.

KEEPING UP

A Kardashian is not to be trifled with.
Each Kardashian, under a leaf-pile
of lush hair, brown and pelted
mantle, contains something hard
and hewn at the core, something
bought and sold in the exchanges
of a difficult spiritual economy.
Each Kardashian is the child of Bedouins
who abandoned her, a crying heap
between hillocks of an empty
landscape, all dirt, then returned to her
quickly, just as soon as that terror
set in. Then they did it again.
Each Kardashian is completely capable
of being alone at night, in fact each lights
herself. Possibly on fire. No two Kardashians
are fully the same, yet they share, isomorphically,
all the memories of one another. One must never
touch the wings of a Kardashian
because the finger will sully
her biological makeup, and she may
never fly again. On the face of each Kardashian
there is something horribly pushed around. Each
Kardashian knows that when she is alone with herself
the world is more quiet than God.
She listens attentively
although she has no ears

and to a Kardashian everything
is manageable, every moment
has its manager. Each Kardashian, when approached
slowly, perhaps through television,
gives off a low electric hum
like waking up thinking the lover is beside you
and then you open your eyes. Each Kardashian
has been defaced by history.
We will have no more Kardashians here.
The town square is empty, only squeak
of hinges on the wind-tugged sign above
the store, which no longer trades
in Kardashian memorabilia. The shelves
are bare, and no one has opinions.
Each Kardashian is accessorized
with opinions, as many as starlings hovering
at sunset, bodies moved in unison of bodies
known to each other only by wingtips,
and now that distance from one another's touch we call
a Kardashian. We are all done up
with anticipation. We are all
aquiver, all Kims. Heaven jostles,
opens wide, drops these women before us.
When speaking about herself
and just desserts each Kardashian's eyes
grow wide and palpable, a new
sexual planet swimming into view.
We are intimidated, but every Kardashian
understands. At night every Kardashian whispers
intimate words to the camera
inside her lover. The camera inside her lover

she put there. Eavesdrop on the intimate words
and you will hear her say: *The empire of culture
is not gone yet. We have still
so much to learn.*

ON THE MEANING OF LOVE

It was an age when these things could happen. I began
by touching her hand, softly, caressing it. I began
by kissing her. I kissed her with my lips
on her mouth. It was inventive. I opened my lips

onto her mouth. I made it clear that I enjoyed this
and she made it clear that she agreed. I opened up
her mouth and put my lips through. I put my tongue through.
I kissed her with my tongue inside her mouth,

but stilly and feeling around. Then I drew it back. Then
I extended one finger into her mouth, feeling where I couldn't
see. Soon it was two. At this point I was thinking
of heraldry, weighty insignia, all its chains and banners.

But I needed more. I worked her lips back and wedged
my hand in, my other hand to follow. Soon
I was bringing things into her mouth with my two hands:
food, some medicines, a photo of a window. Then it was time

to make the great decision. I told her how I felt about her
and what it meant. I told her how the moon
was her reflection, tilted back in crescent, waning wide open.
Then I stepped inside. I brought everything with me

and went hands first. I pressed my back against her palate
and dug my feet in deep and strong. It felt so right I've stayed

ever since. I know she likes it: now and then I ask her
if she wants to say something. And when I think she does,
I dance inside her mouth to make the words.

GRUEN TRANSFER

And I guess there you were
right about the moment
my eyes got stalled in socket
like gum stuck to pavement:

some inner discipline
of the circulation not fully
worked out, some glowing still
in the electrons in the tube, and I

all about the act of doing
a specific thing, this trade
of cash for object, now
become object, all about

that glassy inner elevator
rising up my gorge, the known
and unknown parts of mall
language now stopped

in the parade of self and task
that bears me up and leaves
me here upon the entry floor,
here to walk no more.

Of maps and the obvious
I sing: we, carried over

many miles to arrive
at ample parking, taking

our ticket, the great drive
for cessation of it,
that desire for the target,
the rise and rills of purchase

like a good new blood
felt in the hands, mottled,
thickened, and what is it
we think we touch? It

burgeons like a monolith:
this map, a heavy legend
placed to help
us help ourselves,

its rudiments in colored blocks,
N4, B10, the paths won't spit
us out again, we thought
we came for purpose until purpose

came for us. I like
to think I'm getting
something real good and un-
expected every time I walk in,

slow, get stopped in my tracks.
There is some tenderness

I know that glazes my eyes,
every invisible hand that wants

to show me the way by hiding it.

ON PERSPECTIVE

Farther away the grapes get larger. An ever-expanding lexicon
needs new meanings to form. A baseball moving should do it,
cut up into pieces, not a torture, much like a still-living cow.
Dried, now, in the sunny field, and the sunny field rounded over,
like the breathing belly, against its seams. Squinting,
you nearly grazed the elements. Putting raisins in the bread
allows one to see the space between them expand
in rising, and this for meaning as well. Troubling to admire
the proportional, but try observing the distance between
your nose and your finger each time you bisect it.
The coincidence of these things and now here I am.
Heat leavens evening. Each time approaching meaning
the spaces around me get bigger. As in the field where
the cat-o'-nine-tails switches to cattle. Say what you will
but it takes a lexicon to know one. Fine gloaming coming,
and sun still bright as a baseball. I put three weapons
in front of you and say, choose. And say, what grasps
the grapes will get the juice out. Although the consonants
often mislead the average foreign speaker, bisect is close
to vivisect. And then follow the seams back around
to where you began. Asking for the oven, still warm. Like
a lively stutter. These fingers may menace just as they graze
the breathing belly. Stitched tight in your room, a looking
for the way out, it's just in front of your nose. What
occupies the pared thing, and are we supposed to be
happy in our despair. Seems like we've been here before.
A trouble to admire what's as far as the eye can see. And on it

a last pitch to the distance, alive and looking about. The sun
sinks down below the sightlines, bigger than before,
but darkness doesn't follow.

EIDOLON

Outside the city of wind and rust,
a woman is being pulled up from a white grave.

He has to be careful with her. He has to imagine
a tenderness brush his hands.

Outline of a closed mouth in white sleep. Rising
to horizon, the bolted quiver of wrist.

Her body is mute and made of sugar.

And he must work quickly. He will carry her
to the pool, lay her in water.

Sweet form landing for the last time lets go
of the quick sugar hungers. A thigh touches first

and dissolves. Moments along the granular
hand and neck take on distance, then subside.

He stands back up, tired. Wind will take the rest.

By morning she'll be a flat white cloud.
He'll walk to town behind shoulders,
tasting the body on his fingers.

DISTRACTION

Galloping rush to the other side I feel it
in my ribs. Somewhere the tear is heard
in flesh in seams I think my own. I'm presently

looking on screen at several sites at once
with tabs to help my purpose. I have purpose
until I don't, or used to, and this seems

a reasonable way to pass through the crowd
of an afternoon. Soon I'll know eighteen
things I didn't want to about John Boehner

by way of farm-to-table news and this
video of guinea pig. Hunger productive
in that it draws the body away when mind

cannot. You think you have a plan until
you're busy but with what. It's never bad
to do three things at once if the goal

is not to finish. I really need some
art-school notes on ochre and before
my think-piece privilege injection

a friend to wish us all happy National
Day Day. I see a post, a funny term
for the stationary, something fixed

sempiternally, a stake in the ground or flag
to mark territory; but all I mark is not
sure where I just read that though I did

I'm almost certain. The root of distraction
in Latin was *distrahere*, which we know now
is not dissimilar to being drawn and quartered

by horses, the vision that the self can be
in two directions at once pulled, pulling
perhaps the hemispheres of the brain attached

to different bridles toward opposite points,
audience cheering, the thought of con-
demnation so strong we think we're almost

sure we know what we were meant to feel
when the crime was first committed.
We mark our bodies this way and save it

and offer it to others, do you want to
tag Jay Deshpande. My face blazoned
across the mid-afternoon sites of many

sleeping sitting up, faces of the overfull
and foolishly employed, sitting at desks
in states of open plan, we tab

to another and see another do another's
chores and feel vaguely sure this is real
or the point of what we should be doing

but what was it? In old days someone punished us
this way but now we can be relied on to do it
independently. The beauty in the back

some part of my brain knows just what to do
to get me to do nothing ever again.
I scroll dissatisfied, turn and scroll, I am

all for not exactly getting anything
done today. I like the way the zoning out
looks on me. I lost the direction

somewhere along in here, I'm torn between
the airspeed of the parakeet and where this storm
makes landfall, and I hear the last I hear

will be the hooves on sand to take me to
a most sure of other places, which is me when
in several parts and not discerning anything.

DAEDALUS

It's a blessing to construct
a device so perfectly
fulfilling its promise
can't find its way out.

BEWILDERMENT

At a break in the forest, he saw a wide lake
frozen white and silent like some distant palazzo.
Nothing but dark necks rising from it.

A hundred black horses, heads studding the surface.

Through the ice he couldn't see their bodies.
As if the cold had taken those completely.

The total stillness. Then the wind, lifting one mane.

Near the lake's edge, some few were caught
where they had risen horribly on the backs
of one another, trying to touch land. Each eye

open wide and stricken with terror.
Now, only the sound of the wind. Their shadows
doubling each darkness onto the ice.

And every head was turned to face the shore.

INNER
EAR

We're playing make-believe when the cloud-piercer walks in,

still wet and wrapped in the blue vines.

He looks me directly in the eye

then opens up his mouth.

A small porcelain castle slips off his tongue

and he hands it to me.

No.

It is an organ of sex without gender.

It is the teeth of my enemy,

who I will not yet meet for twenty years.

CHET BAKER

When two people love each other it's a sign
there are parts of the map we save for silence.
But that's not Saturday night.
Your city puts its makeup on. It looks
at itself in the gun-mirror. It looks like it feels
when a great decade presses down
you shut your eyes.
You shut your eyes and think of going home,
of getting tucked in
by your animal companion.
Of being absolutely unrelenting about just one thing.

CHET BAKER

Your mother enters the story at its far end.

She comes toward you but must stop over and over.

Each time she stops,

she says something very loudly about the water

but you can't hear it.

You can hear the water, though.

The water is telling you please not to fall asleep.

By the time your mother reaches you it is night.

An emblem appears in the sky.

She says she hasn't seen it since the day you were born.

CHET BAKER

For hours I went up and down the block,

trying to decide whether to go in.

Eventually the wind came up and the traffic thinned.

I put my hand to the door.

Inside was an empty room, empty but for a white table

with a body floating above it.

It was my body floating above it.

I put on my glasses and stepped closer.

It was a stone being skipped and all its leaps at once.

It was a book being written in the process of being torn apart.

CHET BAKER

Two sisters decide to confess
all the things they ever did to harm one another.
They spend seasons making the list.
They write it out in black ink
on black paper. Look at it closely, it's
the savage lesson in a lullaby
we tell ourselves repeatedly
no one's ever going to get hurt.

CHET BAKER

It was about to call you by your real name.
No, your other name.
The one that sounds like the rose of a woman's hair
coming dangerously undone.
The one that's etched in the rhetoric of a mouth avoiding
certain sounds. That's what it wanted to call you.
When it forgets the words it asks
you lie somewhat nearer the scalpel.

CHET BAKER

I know one house on the block is touched
by none of the others.
Unlettered, forever strikes me
as the terrible sound the bone makes
when it first kisses air.
All these years raving:
I was a bicycle on fire in a field
marked out for ghosts.
I was the light on that field, growing mild.
Or the thing some people call success
when there's blood in their mouths.

CHET BAKER

The subway brings you to a room
where you are alone with the woman you used to love.
As you sit there unable to speak
she takes you in her arms
and softly lists all the things that have hurt you
in the last three years.
She strokes your hair and she lists them out in order.
When she is finished you can't see her.
It is completely dark and nothing touches you.
You make shapes with your mouth.
You start to smell a history of smoke.

CHET BAKER

You are going to get better.
You are going to clean the rooms
you walk in dust to dark with but your feet still know it.
You are going to be alone with the body
but only for a minute, someone a shoulder
asks over to watch it we are coming back
differently. You are going to get free.

CHET BAKER

There is a small piece of a castle I keep
that keeps me up at night.
One night it reaches out to touch me
and stencil me with its rules.
I drink them down and deep like famous milk.
And now I am not alone.
Now I see the world breathing.
When I do sleep, I hear the consultants talking.
Saying, we'll have to take him to the bridge.

CHET BAKER

The way someone loves me in the dictionary
is as good as any other. I keep looking
for the proper sun to lace my tongue with.
To burn on me for days.
There's an arrogance when the solo hits:
it's the paginated clamor of car crashes
I keep beside me in the bed.
But I always knew I would be lucky.
I have that thing about my heart.

CHET BAKER

I am Chet Baker's one son
in a white t-shirt
and a black heart
and a beautiful face
not knowing any more what I can love
still speaking resolutely like the sound
of a body dropped in the river
still picking up feverishly the rain
wrapping in newsprint
a gift that someone gave me
it is a gift that I can't look at
it is a gift that I must carry

A GOLD BEAST COME TO REST BEHIND ME

ELEGY FOR A YEAR

I'm going to get drunk tonight, in my home, by the side
of my own side, like a fishing village preparing for winter.

I'm going to unite myself with the hair of every former tenant
of my disconsolate thirty-year form. Something stifles

through the tender-grass. Strokes the pond on its hot slept heart.
I reach for my ghosts like Horatio. When I wake up again,

the day will have a saddle on. Even though it's not yet sun o'clock.
Flashback, New Year's: my friend drops the hatchet on the hatchet

on love, and I can't ignore the clacking in my shirt pocket
any longer. I reach up with a hand of milk: inside I find in threes

the small cool stones I meant to leave on the shelf of a memory
of the persons I lost. It's what you do when someone's family tree

falls in the forest and no one is around.
April rises like a giddy burn, its fists of one night

trading badges with the constables of the next.
I want to be shorn again as much as I want to never go back.

When someone lets me speak my anchor-song to Central Park,
spraying enormous air over the summer-ready company,

I feel briefly guilty. The crank I turn the world with
is such a hot thing. It uses the lungs of others like a coal-engine.

And it is for this reason that tonight I will be alone.
With my madness. With my menu of hors-d'oeuvres

with dug-out cores. And when I wake up again
to the tune of another year older, a clock in the sink,

I'll see me as the remarkable being at the center
of a flat myth elephants think of as they sleep

on the talkative plains. I'll be there among the tusks inside of me.
With the thing I hold that holds the thing I need.

TO BODY WHAT'S AROUND ME

Stomach feels cloyed and trembling, often the day
is trembling, often I am small step on a branch pressing up,
then giving up, and still with walking on. These are the days

in which you come to me, not to say exquisite but no less
a vessel for it: you here, with amazingly attached arms. I am never
interior but a shaken thing. I remember

the field on top of the hill that approached a line, wooden
how it was not approached, and this light damage of childhood

is somehow meaning now. I know the grasses
I wouldn't walk on, and the more real ferns. Meaning now.

When partial I am somehow looking most directly at you,
and this happens to be frequent, and you'll never understand.
But you see a perhaps, and I, I hold you for it.

Still the hill's inside, with its one sun going down.
Stillside the hill, and the touching never stops.

BURN

The afternoon drains out of us
and we are still here, still August, still slick
from this rain that convicted the sky and left
and only the painted spurs of fire escapes
recall any of that sensation, the hours
next to each other in the rumpled bed
and making conversation, a small laugh,
a story, it's forgotten now and no one hears.
No one cares for the heretic shapes
my moonlight makes, yes I swear I did it
and acted alone, I saw the outside edge
of your mouth turned to speak and was afraid
like a knife about to fall off a desk
but no sound came out, and I am still here.

SOLVE FOR X

You've got a problem
but it's touching you
in all the conceivable places
you shy away from light.
I grew up a coward
on a small vestige of flesh
farmed and loved
until it wasn't
but the scar-harvest.
Tender imagining your face
I am ready to burn
but then I wake up
and have to tongue
my solitude again.
I said I have to
tongue my solitude
again, were you listening?
It is possible
I have crowned you
with that fearfully
intimate otherness
like dangling the garment
of an ex-lover
on a fence at the edge
of my skin—I am accomplice
to all that stupefied terrain.

UNTETHER

When I lose you, there will be a great earthly sound
risen from the lake, and I will look at the lake,
its quiet ducks, its skittered, bathing trees,
its last light slipping from the water-map—and know
this sound comes not from it, but me.

NEED

After they had left the room, we set the body on its side.
The door closing, we watched the pink sheen on his shoulder
turn to gray. Then, with hands that had not eaten for days
we pressed into him, peeling back the skin and the seen
layers. We took our time. After the first few hours
he was red and coarse; longer, later, he was a geography.
And we began to look for the organ that had brought us here,
something unseen and hidden, perhaps behind the lungs
or under the turning muscle that ribbons the hip
or between the genitals and the stomach—or everywhere,
an intelligence to feed the rest of this dormant kingdom.
In the end we had to concede the body to its silence.
But giving up and turning him back over we suddenly caught sight
of what we wanted: that shining presence, like a tree carved in rock
that flowered with his former breathing. Carried on the sound.
It was here that he produced his desires, and we could see
as we looked closer each of them still spawning from those minor shoots:
a moment over a breathless woman whose face was turned away,
the long road furling over hills into the Welsh distance,
his body sudden with air when someone knocked him down
—and children, the free moon in the eye of his one son
its own private accomplishment. These he had kept inside
himself for years, seeding all the rest, holding
the greedy tumble of his being in one place, together, no wars
inside the village. We put him back where he belonged.
Locking the door and walking home
our hands were luminous in the crisp winter light.

ECLOGUE WITH ANIMUS

Now as I'm without you, I walk this wood
sweat-locked and ravening. Golden hours
fall deadly on the bark, the rotted moss. I see
the hill; the hill speaks to me; it tells me
I am home and not at home, here and going
forward. The dryness in my mouth defends it
as these buds, the figures in a flower-speech,
fall to my hair and want to come back with me,
back to rooms where I take parts of you
with eyes half shut and put my hands to mission
to put it all together. With the pieces in union
they are as leaves, and I read on them: the body
cries out when it learns it is here for love,
and is the stranger for this calling.

LETTER FROM THE CHURCH
OF THE BROKEN BODY

Repentant,

       You know the way the canyon picks up light—
not all at once, but with a speed the dust
can only call swelling: first one trough,
then another, day leeching into each thing
separately, like how the eye falls on cells
of an overripe persimmon, knowing where
the thumb can feel that give and lush
before the knife can have its way. Sorrow
follows each of us since June. The fowl
move around the feed like obsessives,
like believers in the constant fear
of being touched. When we go to gather
spices from the fields now, we tug at the plants
with hungry gloves. Skyward, the horizon
each day makes shoulders as though
someone said our village will never
be loved again, and the air complied.
It is colder, but in the crackle of ozone
we think our noses work better. Just
yesterday, Timothy awoke and told
the strangest thing: how at vespers he raised
his eyes, looking out the window, and saw
coming from the face of every denizen
these blue spirits, smokelike and lissome,
billowing out from the eyes, the mouth,

the nose, the ears, every gap in the flesh
that would let them. They seemed to thrill
on air, but none of the people noticed
what rose and tangled. After telling us
Timothy became very ill, and we had
to remove several of his limbs for fear
of his added recalcitrance. The work
was stiff and brutal, but these are such days
when we must act according to laws and live
often outside ourselves. Timothy understands
our ways, as you do, too. You know we each
keep a secret inside our flesh, it weathers
with the darker seasons, and we wait
for the moment when the body has weakened—
that sign its great love can be taken from us.
The nights may be cooler, but in afternoon
no parishioner speaks of pain any longer,
every one hears a sound like rain
clarifying her prayers, seeding his mind
with new heat, great fervor, a readiness.

CRUELTY

No one keeps full company with the knives.
The blazes along the trail become occasionally
wan, bled-out, unreadable. The executioner
polishes also the lemons that grow so brightly
behind his country home. When her father
told her about the affair, at first she felt gratitude
to know he was not dying. The mind
reaches the thornbush some time later.
And the thornbush: the months of it,
the clattering. Legend reports the factual
possibility that a woman can tear the flesh
off her own body, piece by piece, but
accommodatingly. That a man can wake up
on the hillside of his sixth decade and find
his tongue dry from the words: *they should
take out my eyes for what I've done*. These actions
are easier for the human animal than turning
with kindness to one's reflection. And still
we each somehow live in peace and the provisional
version of self-love. The mechanism not broken,
though rarely developed into muscle. When the knife
enters, it is then we are most in this partnership
with one another. The fugue is one of mirroring
and mud. And we must be good to each other,
very good, grateful as the downwind wolves.

THE MUSIC IS SWEET
WHEN IT'S STUCK INSIDE OF US

Up into lilacs or perhaps
lighter evening on the fresh
wings of obliteration I think

about breaking my voice
the way a desperate man
might snap his own bone

the arm in the hand
a wayward angel
a small orange bird

I lose speech for a moment
I am already back
in the lake district

ON SPEAKING QUIETLY WITH MY BROTHER

You who threw the rock at the back of my head
  as hard as you could at four because you thought
this was how to make a stone skip on the ocean,
  I have watched you in the dark of a yard
where we can only see each other by a lamp left on
  some rooms away. We can see only
one another's chin. Soon, you will stay up
  through the night after I fall
into a laughing sleep. Two moths dust
  the same screen for remembered light.
We have all been removed from the lyrics, brother,
  our names will be stricken from the papers.

When I think of you and me and recall some
  adolescent sunrise, standing on rooftops,
blue still the island but the bowl of it about
  to fill with light, it is perhaps strange and horrible
to know one day one of us will die
  and the other will be alive, volume turned up,
his mouth now weighing twice as much.
  We cannot be excused from this
device of road and harrow, from this weight
  we heft and heave. So, you will be the sister.
And I will be the sister. And you—
  you are about to give me my words.

DREAM OF DISCONSOLATE STRANGERS

In the dream you were etching something and it was
        to be, later, me. And so we go on.
    Water, moving, makes its own hollow.

We teach ourselves, luck, and look: a moving retrospective
        on, say, the thirty most recent nights.
    These I carry along with me, and no more

are we able to break. From this as from land, from ocean.
        At times we are touching and mostly
    not. Mostly we are talking

and not hearing presences
        in our blood. Listen: a man can apologize for only
    so much. Not for the willows, their bends,

not for the wavetips, each time inventing new forms,
        each time collapsing in a new hollow of self,
    hollowed for holding. We keep from each other

just so much as begs belief. Just so much
        as light, trestled in leaves descending,
    endures a scampered play. In time this too moves on.

In time there is shadow and also
        coolness. In time silence makes its own river
    run through what has become our common day. And revoking,

never letting things come over, never
                letting blood. What forgiveness takes
          it takes away. We are on riverbanks, brushed-up,

shored from movement, in shock, shuddering.

IN TRUTH I DO NOT SUFFER

In truth I do not suffer,
making shapes with the tongue
in my mind. What is pleasure
asks of the tiniest filament
in the tiniest bulb, tonight
I want you to light every part of me.
I guess I'll now admit there was wind
like none other, and the city's
swirl constant, so constant, to tease
me to the shore. Flailing sounds rage
in the brain not awake for another
few strokes yet, and the sun sets up
its frequency of plea. No less.
I have done with the gallery,
done with the jowls. I have walked
sunrise through villages a taut harp
and cold at the side of my structure,
but I believe in my structure, its yes.
It is true there are good boats here,
and every hill a chapel bears
to boast me to the north. I think
some lake wants the best for me.
But in truth I do not suffer,
I am the wash and angle of all
alternative and I have
seen what I came here to see.

BRIGHTLY

Window open:
a fullness in the gingko
carried over continents
maybe saying
how long could I live
on just water
and the sight of you
each blossom entirely alone
finds a sweeter winter
in its disposition
and the sky clouds
with uplift

ACKNOWLEDGMENTS

Thank you to the editors of the following publications where these poems first appeared, sometimes in earlier forms:

Bodega: "Brightly," "The Secret Life"

Boxcar Poetry Review: "Apologia Pro Vita Sua"

Boston Review: "On Voluptuousness at la Fontana di Trevi," "Porn," "Elegy for a Year"

cream city review: "Eidolon," "The Music Is Sweet When It's Stuck Inside of Us"

death hums: "Forest : Trees"

The Fanzine: "Chet Baker [When two people love each other it's a sign]," "Chet Baker [For hours I went up and down the block]," "Chet Baker [I know one house on the block is touched]," "Chet Baker [The subway brings you to a room]"

Handsome: "Dramatis Personae or In This House A Single Thread," "To Body What's Around Me"

Hot Metal Bridge: "On Perspective"

HTMLGiant: "Strength"

La Petite Zine: "Threatening Weather"

Linebreak: "Prairie Song with Jack Palance"

Narrative: "Keeping Up," "On the Meaning of Love"

No, Dear: "Bewilderment"

Phantom Limb: "But First You Have to Close Your Eyes"

Prelude: "Distraction," "Letter from the Church of the Broken Body"

Poem-a-Day: "On Speaking Quietly with My Brother"

Sixth Finch: "Klaxon"

Spork: "Inflorescence"

Vinyl: "Dream of Disconsolate Strangers," "Tracing"

✦ ✦ ✦

Both this book and I owe tremendous thanks to an untold number of people who provided love, encouragement, and inspiration over a long process. I name many here but I can think of many more.

Thanks in the highest to KMA Sullivan—a fantastic editor and an amazing heart—and to the YesYes team. I am so grateful for your insights and your advocacy.

Thanks to my teachers at Harvard and Columbia, especially Timothy Donnelly, Jorie Graham, Josh Bell, Lucie Brock-Broido, Peter Richards, Eamon Grennan, Mark Bibbins, Mónica de la Torre, Marjorie Welish, and Mark Strand. And to other guides: thank you Peter Sacks, Sven Birkerts, Beth Harrison, Sue Mendelsohn, Aaron Ritzenberg, John Charles Smith, David Foster, Douglas Fricke, Alice Quinn, Stefania Heim, and Idra Novey. Special thanks to Joanna Klink and to Diana Al-Hadid.

Thank you to the extraordinary community of writers and artists I am lucky to have in my life, including Marina Blitshteyn, Elizabeth Clark Wessel and Mårten Wessel, Iris Cushing, JC Longbottom, Julia Guez, Montana Ray, Nalini Edwin and Joshua Daniel Edwin, Sam Ross, Hilary Vaughn Dobel, Courtney Kampa, Amber Galeo, Gerard Coletta, Lindsay Turner, Morgan Parker, Molly Rose Quinn, Lynne Potts, Jason Boulanger, Natalie Eilbert, Kelly Forsythe, and Adam Scheffler. For both their kinship and their insights into this manuscript as it developed, I am especially grateful to Ben Purkert, Sasha Fletcher, Kirkwood Adams, and E.C. Belli.

Deep love and gratitude to Daniel Anderson, Victor Hu, Roberto Michelassi, Munia Jabbar, David Forbes, Fazal Yameen, Nick Kojucharov, Kevin Velez and the whole Velez family, Charles Bisbee, Chris Dalton, Kate Walker,

Annelisa Pedersen, Drew Heckathorn, Will Pattie and Andrea Sledd, Fiona Kaye, Elizabeth Ballard, and Raydene Salinas. This book would not have been possible without Diksha Basu. Thank you Daniel Greenspun. Thank you Gerald Schorin. Thank you Peter Malamud Smith, Alexandra Hannibal, and Kirk Reardon. Your influence and inspiration is felt throughout these pages.

Thank you to those organizations and individuals who have provided support for my writing: Lesley Williamson at the Saltonstall Foundation for the Arts; at the Key West Literary Seminar, Miles Frieden, Arlo Haskell, and Billy Collins; at Kundiman, Joseph Legaspi and Wo Chan; and the team at *Narrative*. And especially to *WatchTime* Magazine, to Joe Thompson and to Norma Buchanan.

To my parents, Rebecca Schorin and Rohit Deshpande, for the depths of their support and their understanding—all of my love. And to my brother Neil, for being witness, partner, and hero. The three of you are my most constant sources of wonder.

VINYL 45s

A PRINT CHAPBOOK SERIES

After by Fatimah Asghar

Pepper Girl by Jonterri Gadson

Bad Star by Rebecca Hazelton

Still, the Shore by Keith Leonard

Please Don't Leave Me Scarlett Johansson by Thomas Patrick Levy

No by Ocean Vuong

POETRY SHOTS

A DIGITAL CHAPBOOK SERIES

Nocturne Trio by Metta Sáma

[ART BY MIHRET DAWIT]

Toward What Is Awful by Dana Guthrie Martin

[ART BY GHANGBIN KIM]

How to Survive a Hotel Fire by Angela Veronica Wong

[ART BY MEGAN LAUREL]

The Blue Teratorn by Dorothea Lasky

[ART BY KAORI MITSUSHIMA]

My Hologram Chamber Is Surrounded by Miles of Snow by Ben Mirov

[IMAGES BY ERIC AMLING]